BLOODSUCKERS

MOSQUITOES

Hungry for Blood

BARBARA A. SOMERVILL

PowerKiDS press

New York

Published in 2008 by The Rosen Publishing Group, Inc.
29 East 21st Street, New York, NY 10010

First Edition

Editors: Geeta Sobha and Joanne Randolph
Book Design: Dean Galiano
Layout Design: Greg Tucker
Photo Researcher: Nicole Pristash

Photo Credits: Cover © David Sharf/Getty Images; pp. 5, 11, 13, 15, 17 © Shutterstock.com; p. 7 by Janice Carr/CDC/Paul Howell; p. 9 by James Gathany/CDC; p. 19 © Getty Images; p. 21 © age fotostock/SuperStock.

Library of Congress Cataloging-in-Publication Data

Somervill, Barbara A.
  Mosquitoes : hungry for blood / Barbara A. Somervill. — 1st ed.
      p. cm. — (Bloodsuckers)
  Includes index.
  ISBN-13: 978-1-4042-3802-2 (library binding)
  ISBN-10: 1-4042-3802-6 (library binding)
  1. Mosquitoes—Juvenile literature. I. Title.
  QL536.S64 2008
  595.77'2—dc22
                                                    2006103371

Manufactured in the United States of America

CONTENTS

LITTLE FLY

Every Fourth of July, your parents, grandparents, aunts, uncles, and cousins get together to enjoy the day. Everyone spends the day eating and playing games. As the Sun begins to set, you feel something on your arm. Quick! You squash it, and a smear of blood appears. It is summertime, and the mosquitoes are biting.

The word *mosquito* is Spanish for "little fly." Mosquitoes are actually related to flies. The big difference between them is that flies eat the food at the party, while mosquitoes prefer to dine on the people.

Only female mosquitoes are bloodsuckers. The males feed only on plants.

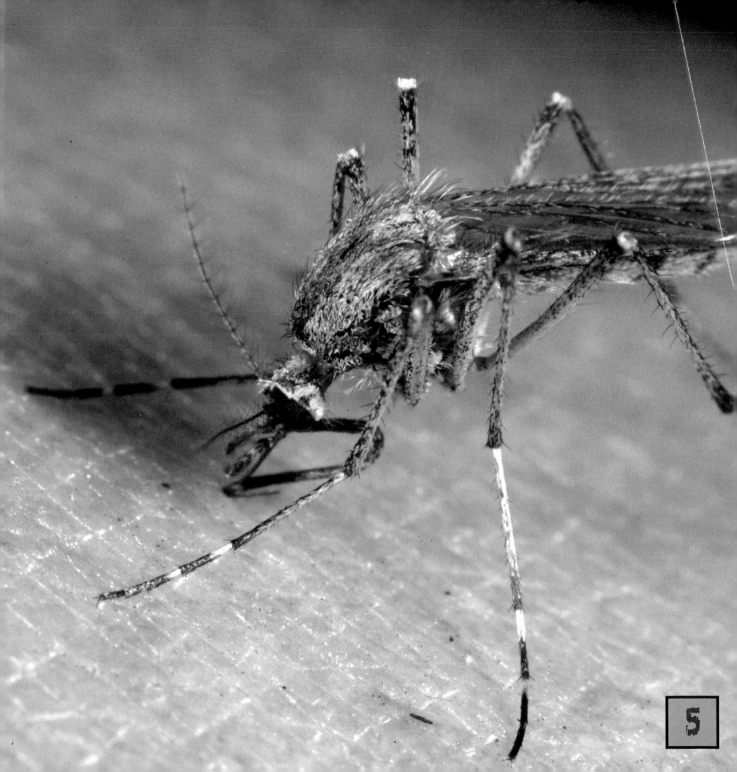

MEET THE MOSQUITO

Mosquitoes are insects. They have three basic body parts. These parts are the head, **thorax**, and **abdomen**. The head has eyes, a mouth, and a brain. A mosquito's **compound** eyes have many tiny lenses. The eyes see movement anywhere nearby. Mouthparts called palps allow the mosquito to feed. Females also have a **proboscis**, a tube used to suck blood.

The thorax has two wings, six legs, and **muscles** to make the legs and wings work. The abdomen is where a mosquito breaks down its food.

This is a close-up look at a mosquito's head. You can see the compound eye, the antennae, and the feathery-looking palps.

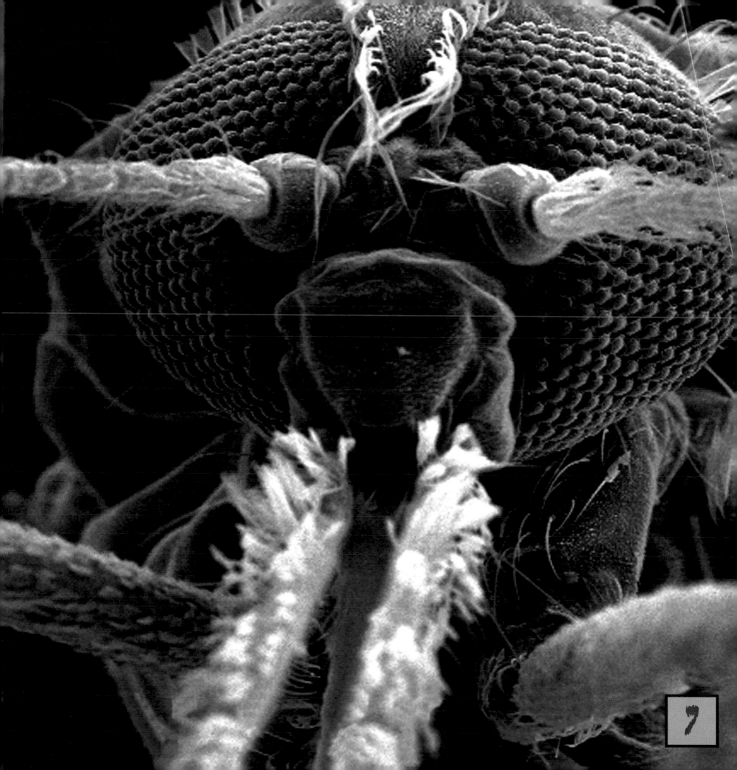

KINDS OF MOSQUITOES

There are about 2,700 **species** of mosquitoes throughout the world. About 150 species live in North America. Most of those mosquitoes belong to one of three family groups.

Aedes (ay-EE-deez) mosquitoes lay their eggs where there is water from floods. Anopheles (an-OF-eh-leez) mosquitoes lay eggs in permanent lakes, ponds, or still water. Culex (KYOO-leks) mosquitoes lay eggs in quiet standing water in places such as birdbaths, flowerpots, and old tires. They are the most common species in cities.

Aedes mosquitoes, like this one, are strong fliers that generally bite at dawn or sunset. This mosquito has just bitten a person's hand.

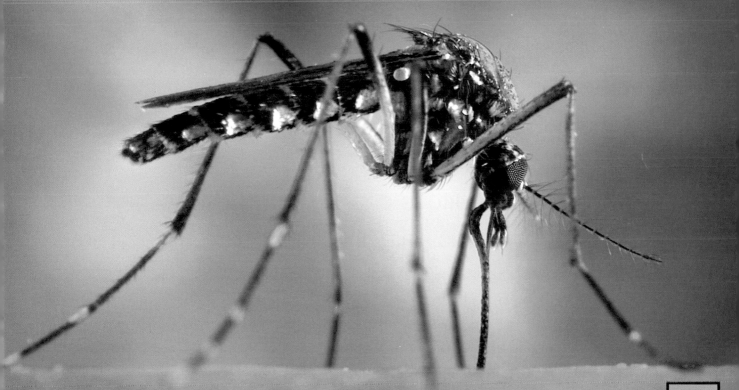

9

HOME, WET HOME

Mosquitoes live where there is standing water. They lay their eggs in water, and their **larvae** live in water. Where you find freshwater and warm weather, you will find mosquitoes.

That means mosquitoes live in forests, meadows, and backyards. They like lakes, ponds, slow-moving rivers, and puddles. They will lay eggs in tubs, buckets, wheelbarrows, swimming pools, and your dog's outside water dish.

Although mosquitoes can be found everywhere except the Antarctic, they like warmer weather. They do not bite at temperatures colder than 50° F (10° C).

Swamps, like this one, make good homes for mosquitoes. There is always a lot of standing freshwater in which they can lay their eggs.

WHAT MOSQUITOES EAT

Both male and female mosquitoes drink plant **nectar** for food. Males never bite animals. Females, however, need a blood meal to supply the **protein** needed for their eggs.

Although human blood is easier to get, mosquitoes also bite dogs, cats, birds, and other animals. When the female bites, she injects a liquid into the wound to prevent the blood from **clotting**. The blood flows freely as the female sucks. A female drinks blood just before laying her eggs.

A mosquito has found a spot to feed between this cat's eyes. Once she drinks her fill of blood, this mosquito will find a place to lay her eggs.

HUNTING FOR BLOOD

Mosquitoes have many ways to find food. The mosquito can find carbon dioxide and lactic acid in the air. These are waste gases given off when animals breathe.

Mosquitoes can also see different colors. A bright red shirt stands out against green grass. When the human wearing the shirt moves, the mosquito sees it. To a mosquito, movement means something is alive and may be a source of blood.

Warm-blooded animals, such as humans and dogs, give off body heat. A mosquito zooms in on that heat because it probably means food.

THE BITER GETS BITTEN

Mosquitoes are food for dozens of animal species. In a lake or pond, mosquito fish and guppies feed on eggs and larvae. A hungry mosquito fish eats up to 50 larvae in an hour.

In the air, dragonflies and birds feed on mosquitoes. However, bats have the greatest mosquito appetite. Bats can eat about 600 to 1,000 mosquitoes in an hour.

Some animals and plants trap mosquitoes. Spiders use their webs to trap mosquitoes. Pitcher plants and Venus flytraps are plants that eat insects like mosquitoes.

This bird, called a shrike, eats insects like mosquitoes. Birds and other animals help keep the number of mosquitoes down.

17

MOSQUITOES AND ILLNESSES

Mosquitoes are known to spread illnesses. Some illnesses spread by mosquitoes are deadly, such as malaria, yellow fever, dengue, and West Nile virus. Millions of people around the world get sick with malaria and dengue every year. In countries where these illnesses are common, the government sprays **pesticides** to cut the mosquito population.

The female mosquito bites a person or an animal that is ill. When the mosquito bites its next victim, that person or animal may get sick.

This man is spraying pesticides to kill mosquitoes carrying the West Nile virus. In the United States, West Nile virus is one of the illnesses spread by mosquitoes.

19

THE LIFE OF A MOSQUITO

The mosquito life cycle is made up of four stages, or parts. These stages are egg, larva, **pupa**, and adult. Females lay 40 to 400 eggs. Eggs usually break open quickly but can last over the winter.

When the eggs break open, larvae come out. They eat, grow, and shed their skin. They grow and shed four times before they enter the pupal stage.

Pupae, called tumblers, change into adult mosquitoes. This takes one to four days. Adults quickly mate to carry on the species. Males live only a few days. Females may live days, weeks, or through the winter.

Mosquito larvae, also called wrigglers, look like worms squirming in the water. The first three mosquitoes in this picture are larvae. The last one is a pupa.

CONTROLLING MOSQUITOES

If you know when mosquitoes bite, you can keep yourself from being attacked. Wear long sleeves, long pants, and socks when you are in places with mosquitoes. Use an insect **repellent**.

Dawn and dusk are the times when mosquitoes are out. Plan your outdoor activities around those times. Have screens on windows and doors and hold suppertime activities inside.

Get rid of standing water in buckets, birdbaths, and other things that can hold water. Mosquitoes will always bite. It is their nature. Be smart and you might keep from being bitten.

GLOSSARY

abdomen (AB-duh-mun) The lower part of an insect's body.

clotting (KLAHT-ing) Thickening.

compound (KOM-pownd) Made up of two or more different things.

larvae (LAHR-vee) Insects in the early life stage in which they have a wormlike form.

muscles (MUH-sulz) The parts of the body that make the body move.

nectar (NEK-tur) The sweet liquid of flowering plants.

pesticides (PES-tuh-sydz) Chemical substances that kill pests, such as rodents and insects.

proboscis (pruh-BAH-sus) The long, tube-shaped mouthpart of an insect.

protein (PROH-teen) A natural substance needed by animals for growth.

pupa (PYOO-puh) The insect stage during which larva grows into an adult.

repellent (rih-PEH-lunt) Something that keeps animals or insects away from a person or object.

species (SPEE-sheez) One kind of living thing.

thorax (THOR-aks) The middle part of an insect, crustacean, or spider.

INDEX

WEB SITES

Due to the changing nature of Internet links, PowerKids Press has developed an online list of Web sites related to the subject of this book. This site is updated regularly. Please use this link to access the list:
www.powerkidslinks.com/bsu/mosq/